FINGERPRINTS OF Love AND War

Fingerprints of Love & War

Copyright © 2018-2020 Edward L. Holmes II.

All rights reserved. No part of this publication may be reproduced, distributed, or transmitted in any form or by any means, including photocopying, recording, or other electronic or mechanical methods, without the prior written permission of the publisher.

ISBN-13: 978-0-578-66381-4

Acclivity Publishing

Cover & Interior Design
Edward L. Holmes II

Illustrated by
Robin M. Bandy

FINGERPRINTS OF Love AND War

Edward Holmes

ACCLIVITY
PUBLISHING

For the incredible grace of Almighty God

which turns the most irreparable hearts

into beautiful masterpieces.

...For you...

CONTENTS

FINGERPRINTS
CH. 1 INTRO 1

The Image 7
Meek Mister Mayfield 13
Poor Traits 19
Mystery Victor: E 23
She Smiles in the Dark 27
Lion's Tooth 31

LOVE
CH. 2 INTRO 37

Compass 43
Musings of the Master 47
Love on Display 51
Harmony 55
Through the Loop 59
Senseless 63
Why the Kettle Sings 67

WAR
CH. 3 INTRO 73

Focus 77
Edge 81
Last Word 89
Still Water 93
Wrinkles 97
Temperance 101
Fetter Pillows 105

Final Word 109

FINGERPRINTS

Chapter 1
Fingerprints

First, you need to understand that who you are is what you do. You know, the surface-level, skin-deep details. It starts with your education... a good one. Study hard and walk with your degree(s) in hand so you can land a suitable career to sustain your future family. That's right! You're getting married soon because time waits for no man (neither do potential partners). That reminds me... you've been due for a new weight loss trend to follow. Your social presence will accrue more organic followers if you just trim a little fat from the Christmas hog... if... you know what I mean. More cash, less sags, more hashtags and travel bags, baby! The journey towards self-actualization starts here today! Go get 'em!

Something More

This septic sauce of monotony is the lifestyle the world feeds us through a rubber IV. We lay back and take in its tyrannical toxin, conforming to "what we've always been taught." Surely there has to be more to life than simple survival. Jesus said He came to give us abundant life (John 10:10), so why at times does it seem so meaningless? The Lord said He came to prosper us, to give us a hope and a future (Jeremiah 29:11), so why are many holding four years of college education, yet unemployed? He saw that it wasn't good for Adam to be alone and gave him a wife (Genesis 2:18), so "why am I still flying solo?" You say that You're a God who hears, so surely You've heard my cries of heartache!"

I don't claim to have all the answers life holds but with the utmost confidence I can say that you (yes, YOU) were created to be unique and His mission, if you choose to accept it (Romans 10:9), will fit like a glove to your life. It will be greater than your career, more satisfying than your wildest dreams and wilder than any party you tried to hold in your dorm, with or without the pizza. I'm talking about living out your unique purpose for living as designed by your Creator!

Purpose

What if I told you that you were created with a specific plan in mind, would you believe me? If I told you that you've impacted lives that you may never meet, would you deny me? Perhaps if I told you there exists nothing in the universe exactly like you, would you agree? Just as the prophet Jeremiah was called before birth, so have we been appointed. "So, you're saying I'm a unique individual, created by God, with a specific purpose. That's great and all, I get it, but how do I know if I'm walking in the divine will of God? How can I be sure that I'm not missing the mark? For us to realize our fullest potential, we have to realize who our Creator is.

"For we are God's masterpiece. He has created us anew in Christ Jesus, so we can do the good things He planned for us long ago."
Ephesians 2:10 (NLT)

EDWARD HOLMES

Opening Our Eyes

We are the Father's masterpieces, but we can't walk in the fullness of His plans until our hearts are fully yielded to Him. I'm reminded of Saul of Tarsus, a man who later contributed two-thirds of the New Testament as the Apostle Paul, sought to persecute the church. It wasn't until his eyes beheld the image of the resurrected Christ in radiant splendor that Saul's entire life turned upside down. Blinded by the light, wrapped up in sheer humility, he waited in Damascus for God's next directive. A man named Ananias, who Saul later describes as godly and deeply devoted to the law (Acts 22:12) was used of God to deliver Saul his sight, calling and baptism. God is omnipotent as Creator of all things. He could have given Saul these three blessings right there in Damascus, yet He chose to use man to carry out His purpose. To be a partaker of a greater work is His ultimate desire for you.

Fingerprints

So maybe you're like Saul and you're waiting to have that interception of God to shatter the monotony of a temporal life. Maybe you reflect Ananias and you're desperately waiting for God to use you in ways you could never imagine! During our journey together, remember that your identity lies within the fingerprints of peace, at the right hand of God. You are His handiwork and He is your lifeline. You are the dust behind each nail as a testimony of His careful craftsmanship. He's ready for your next move, are you?

The Image

I used to say "I'm sorry."
I used to never care.
I used to search for something
that was never really there.

I used to view the mirror
disliking what I saw,
believing what they told me,
after that, I took a fall.

And yet, You gazed upon me
looking down with eyes of love.
The way Your love astounds me,
I could never give enough.

You said that I was more than this,
and told me I was strong,
and yet, I had ignored the voice
that loved me all along.

I used to count my stumbles.
I used to tally sin.
I used to hate the way I was
with never "fitting in."

EDWARD HOLMES

I used to view my friends
with so much envy in my eyes
then later view myself at night
with bitter, dark despite.

And yet, You gazed upon me,
looking down with eyes of love.
The way Your love astounds me,
I could never give enough.

You said that I belong to You
and told me I was smart,
and yet I had ignored the voice
that loved me from the start.

So why did you keep loving me,
I fail you every day.
Sometimes I'm just too blind to see
You love me anyway.

I'll never be like "him" or "her"
or "that guy over there"
because You always wake me up
to know I shouldn't care.

FINGERPRINTS OF LOVE & WAR

You love us for the way we are:
naïve and small and odd.
You've made us with a mission,
though we're faulty, You're still God.

Of course, we tend to tumble
and we're ever prone to sink,
we're crafted in Your image,
so much stronger than we think.

So you, my friend with trying faith
and darkness all around,
you're loved far more than you could think.
In Christ, you're safe and sound.

Don't ignore the feeling,
chase this love with all your heart.
He has a plan for you, my friend,
today's your day to start.

> *"You made all the delicate, inner parts of my body and knit me together in my mother's womb. Thank you for making me so wonderfully complex! Your workmanship is marvelous—how well I know it."*
>
> ***Psalms 139:13-14 (NLT)***

Short...Tall...Fat...Skinny...Black...White...Nerdy... These adjectives flow eloquently from the lips of this world. It looks but does not see while wrapping itself in the security of sarcastic labels. Behold! None are exempt from being judged. Even you, oh daring reader, are a victim of society's gavel. The halls of the high school echo your reputation, but never your name. Your colleagues know how well you can fix a problem, but never see the broken man behind the desk. The airwaves of media demand size zero, chiseled abs, no flabs and the newest kicks, but never see the young girl starving herself to "fit in."

That's okay... The term "fearfully" used in the original text is yārē in Hebrew. It is the same type of fear that we see in reference to GOD. No, not fear as in horror, but awe-inspiring reverence! This word is a description of you. Every pore of your skin, every freckle, every scar, God saw you before you were born and called you breath-taking! Woven with such care and concern, you truly WERE fearfully and most wonderfully made. If marvelous are His works, what does that make you?

With that being said, we must walk daily in this type of spiritual revelation! When the Spirit of God dwells within you and I, we're able to experience His gift of discernment. Simply put, we walk in a daily revelation of truth and this includes the truth about who you are and have always been. Don't fall prey to erroneous expectations and false doctrines that focus more on your imperfections, instead, rest in the knowledge that you are loved for who you are, this moment, this instant and forevermore.

He has a plan for you, my friend.
Today's your day to start.

Meek Mr. Mayfield

Meek Mister Mayfield, a master of charity,
verity, valor, and selfless sincerity.
He's an amalgam composed of whatever he
chooses to be, save his own true identity.

Once met a gentleman under an olive tree,
stated, "I've waited for you to draw nigh to me.
Haven't you fingerprints? Take off the mask!
My friend, blending in is a frivolous task."

But yet Mister Mayfield replied unafraid
with a heart that was stolen and crusted with jade,
"I am who I am and that's all whom I'll be.
I live blending in and I love being me."

Meek Mister Mayfield lives gracefully, tastefully,
pacing with pieces of borrowed anatomy:
arms of an artist, an ankle, an eye,
feet of a ruler, three nails from a Guy

whom he met at the park on a bench after dark
with a wrench and a smile, He said, "Come sit a while.
I fix broken things, I make everything new.
I can mend your identity crisis, it's true!"

But yet Mister Mayfield replied fearing harm, with
a tongue made of patchwork with clippings of yarn,
"I am who I am and that's all whom I'll be,
I live blending in and I love being me."

Meek Mister Mayfield, the strong silent type
but he tells all his friends that's he's "rowdy" at night.
He's contradictory; caustic yet calm,
with deep wounds on his hands,
but a psalm on each palm
that he learned from a Man whom he met on the street.
He embraced Mister Mayfield beginning to speak:

"I'm a Carpenter, friend, I can fix broken things.
I'm an expert with nails, but I mend broken wings.
My work never weathers through torrent or breeze.
I'll show you who you truly are if you please..."

FINGERPRINTS OF LOVE & WAR

But yet Mister Mayfield replied rather sore,
with a heart pounding fast in his insecure core,
"I...am who I am... and that's all whom I'll be.
I live blending in and I love being me."

"NO!"

The man spoke with strength as He said,
"You are mine, I am yours,
we are one, never two, never nine.
I love you, I need you, I knit you together.
You're chosen, you're woven, our love cannot sever.
I know who you are, you were made to be more
and I crafted you special and counted each pore.
I know every heartbeat and tally each hair.
I formed you and warmed you with uttermost care.
I AM the I AM and forever will be.
In Christ, you will find your true identity."

> *"So God created human beings in His own image. In the image of God He created them; male and female He created them."*
>
> ***Genesis 1:27 (NLT)***

Who are you? Honestly stop and think for a second... If each of your closest friends went their separate ways, would you have an existential crisis? If unemployment struck your household for a year, what would you call yourself? Is identity found in what you do and who you do it with? Throughout life, my heart wanted to be part of something, but I never lived my own life. My self-proclaimed I.D. read:

Name: None.
State: Confusion.
Blood type: Be Negative.

One of our basic human needs is a desire for community and companionship. In younger years I desired love so much that I found myself mirroring every motion of the masses no matter how murky my heart became. Unfortunately at the end of the day when my head hit the pillows, I still felt incomplete, empty and nameless.

Have you ever felt that way? A duplicated doppelganger donning different demeanors for everyone? Friend, you are not alone. Contrary to this world's belief, God hasn't given up on you yet. You are made in the image of the Almighty (Genesis 1:26) and He has a full life that only you can live. Do you believe that? He already has a plan to mend the brokenness that you've carried with you thus far; wait and see. He is the Healer of the brokenhearted and He binds up their wounds (Psalm 147:3). Your purpose is something that's not bound to a body that will fade away, but rather something imperishable and unique to only you. Don't deny the call. After all, you are the only *you* that He will ever make.

IN CHRIST YOU WILL FIND YOUR TRUE IDENTITY

Poor Traits

If I could plan a painting,
pass the purple, pass the pink,
I would paint upon my future,
brush the lines of what think to be
the proper path of pacing
towards the ends of this or that.
If I do it all myself, I risk another art attack.

Unless I brush up on obedience
and dye to sin each day,
tone my tongue with tact and tenderness
and prime my heart to pray.
Smudge the traits of self-sufficiency,
erase my pompous past,
crop and cut away what's left of me
for God to work, at last.

He can ease all of my weariness,
illuminate my shades,
so, if I could paint my future,

Well...

On second thought I'll wait.

EDWARD HOLMES

He painted every Starry Night
and molded every man.
He colored every raging sea
and blended with His hands.
I'm just a wretched jar of clay
that few can understand,
but Jesus loved me anyway
despite my selfish plans.

I shall not paint my future
nor begin to etch a line.
My life is in the hands of God
The Artist,
my Divine.

> *"I knew you before I formed you in your mother's womb. Before you were born I set you apart and appointed you as my prophet to the nations."*
>
> ***Jeremiah 1:5 (NLT)***

What are you going to be? Who are you? What are your five-year goals? Ten-year goals? What kind of father do you want to be? Half-Windsor or Full-Windsor? These are questions that launch towards us at light-speed since we're old enough to comprehend the process of planning. We're taught to "find ourselves" through discovery and hard work, so I made many plans and ran hard after them. If you had asked me at the age of twelve who I wanted to be, I would have told you that I was *going* to be a successful cartoonist and programmer, living in Silicon Valley with my wife, beach-view home, and six sons. (Try not to judge me.) No plan B. This was it. I graduated with a Bachelor's degree full of programming languages and loads of knowledge... Still single, no sons, and working as an underpaid billboard designer.

One afternoon, I found a man in the 3rd-floor restroom. His visage had defeat solidified in the crevices where smile lines once danced. I leaned in close over the rusted-speckled faucet where fear ran down his cheek. When I asked him who he was, In unison, the mirror and I replied, "I'm not sure."

With the perception of failure, doubt told me that I was a nobody now. "If I'm not who I dreamed to be, then... Who am I?" You see, my issue was that I had for so long hidden my "identity" in things I did, when in all reality, it was found in whose I was (Jeremiah 1:5). God appointed young Jeremiah as a prophet before he was formed. Likewise, there is a specific calling on your life that just might be the furthest thing from your mind. Sometimes it takes us to get our plans out of the way for God to tell us His own plan.

Today, I've found my voice helping others raise theirs. This is more than sufficient to me than all the riches earth could offer. You are more than a masterpiece, drop the paintbrush.

> My life is in the hands of God, the artist, my divine

Mystery: Victor E.

Victor Erroneous, man in the suit,
studded cane, hat of silk, and the swagger to boot
with an animus twisted from mankind's opinion,
he's not who he is; who he is, is mistaken.

The man in the suit with visage incomplete
walks a path down the road, wave an arm, stop and greet
this peculiar fellow adorned in pure white.
Clean and pressed, I confess he's a marvelous sight!

But his stride is all crooked, his arms rather long,
smudges dance on his cheeks since his face has been
drawn and erased several times, but he still marches on
left-left-right move his feet, indecisive and wrong.

The man in the suit never looks straight ahead,
but his head is held high as if nothing to dread!
If a grimace could grace such a face in his chase of the
wind, men would tend to think ill of our friend.

But alas, he pretends every day as he spends
time to straighten his tie. While he walks, does he lie
to the world when he dons different egos at will?
Right-right-left move his feet, yet he marches on still.

EDWARD HOLMES

The man in the suit's a grammatical CHARM!
So benevolent, eloquent, never means harm
with the words (or the lies)
that he paints (so he tries)
to the people, they faint
(when they see through his guise).

But his stutter reflects every step that he takes,
f-f-fearful to trust the decisions he makes.
Never punctual, functional, straight to the point,
walking stiff with cement locking every joint.

Yes, the man in the suit, what a marvel is he!
Ever clean on the outside, pure white and pristine!
Ribboned top-hat of silk, studded cane, pearly teeth.
This man isn't perfect, and neither are we.

> *"Not a single person on earth is always good and never sins."*
>
> ***Ecclesiastes 7:20 (NLT)***

I remember the day I finally surrendered my sword and chose to live in the grace Jesus prepared for me. I yearned to tell everyone about the love I had found and I could feel the Holy Spirit moving me in the midst. It felt wonderful to know that this God I had discounted for so many years was actually true and changing me!

Yes, everything looked great on the outside, through action and word, but my insides were being repaired. No, no, not my organs (those were fine), but the nature of my soul. God was working overtime on past hurts, breaking addiction and old ways while I still struggled by thought. I felt like a hypocrite: seeking a closer walk with the Father, but missing the mark day after day. "Does anyone notice?" "What will they think?" "Does God still care?" These questions were among my many thoughts. His Word tells us that if anyone is in Christ, he is a new creation (2 Corinthians 5:17), and through His Spirit, we are constantly being transformed (2 Corinthians 3:17-18). Like a caterpillar to a butterfly, God's transformation in our lives takes time, so we can't get discouraged when we sin. Not a single person on earth is always good and never sins. Ecclesiastes 7:20 (NLT) This means that no man, however strong, chaste or tactful, is without the capacity to sin. Therefore, we must be watchful and allow the Holy Spirit to work in our lives. Only then will it come to pass.

This story brings us to today where God's transformation process brought the very freedom that I doubted many years back. Where the Spirit of the Lord is, freedom truly resides, and that freedom is available to you! Just let God have His way, and you'll be amazed at who you become. Everything may look perfect and pristine on the outside, but no man is perfect.

> Ribboned top-hat of silk.
> Studded cane. Pearly teeth.
> This man isn't perfect.
> And neither are we.

She Smiles In The Dark

She's like the moon and
the moon never ceases
to glow when the light is before her.

It pleases the heart to be sure
that these shadows decrease when surrounded
and found by such luminous peace

that can pass every bit
of her own understanding
while standing before darkest troubles

demanding her focus. But know this:
she's not overcome, with two eyes
drenched in light from reflecting the Son.

> *"Your eye is like a lamp that provides light for your body. When your eye is healthy, your whole body is filled with light. But when it is unhealthy, your body is filled with darkness."*
>
> ***Luke 11:34 (NLT)***

We can legitimately say that without light-waves entering the eye, we can see nothing. Sounds like a no-brainer, right? When light passes the cornea, enters the pupil, traveling through the lens, our retinas relay information to our brains. This information tells the brain that what we're seeing is actually, well... what we're seeing! Now consider living in a world where no light sources exist, no sun, no fire, no back-lit smartphones with flashlights. Nothing. How immensely dark and cold would our lives be? Furthermore, without universal sight for all mankind, how would we form proper relationships? How could we know what is true and what is not?

Jesus is often metaphorically referenced as the light of the World. This is such a powerful attribution due to the sheer necessity of light to our lives. Consider how much we rely on light sources as humans to function properly. When our bodies are exposed to proper amounts of sunlight, serotonin (the hormone responsible for mood-boosting and feelings of calm.) is released. Low serotonin levels put the human body at risk for depression, anxiety, and negatively altered moods.

With literal light permeating every bit of our lives, we can live, move and thrive as we've been created to do. I believe the same applies to the eyes of a person now filled with the spiritual light and truth of Jesus. Truth allows us to see how priceless we are. Truth expels legalism and works-based faith. Truth shines into our relationships allowing us to see others for who they truly are: worthy of love regardless of. Keep your eyes full of light, my friend and you'll see the beauty for what it is.

> SHE'S NOT OVERCOME.
> WITH TWO EYES DRENCHED IN LIGHT
> FROM REFLECTING THE SON

Lion's Tooth

Sometimes weather-worn sidewalks give birth to
dandelions seeded in earthen wombs
of impossible circumstances.
No matter how arduous the journey,
she will continue to dream and grow
      and grow
           and grow
until her prowess is pronounced;
pushing her past proverbial projections
of her petrifying past before illumination,
and with her head held high, she will
praise the sun. Dirt was her covering,
but never her definition.
Her mission is far too brilliant,
she is far too resilient to be

silenced.

Bloom is what she was created to do.
      Bloom is what she will.

> *"You are altogether beautiful, my darling, beautiful in every way."*
>
> ***Song of Solomon 4:7 (NLT)***

"How beautiful!" She exclaimed as she clutched a stunning bouquet of gold close to her heart. Four, five, six… probably a dozen of the brightest blooms you'd ever see. At least that's what he would tell you if you asked him. She placed them in the kitchen, only for a time, to let him know just how proud she was of the gift. Even if they were dandelions, in her eyes these were the most precious she'd ever seen.

My mother has been and always will be a central focal point of encouragement, discipline, and beauty in our family. It was commonplace for her to find ways to lavish her three children with gifts even when the means were not there. I remember the day I decided to show her just how much I appreciated her hard work with a bouquet of dandelions! Yes, dandelions, a handful of weeds tied up with grass was fitting for a queen of her caliber, no doubt. Though these weeds were on full siege of our lawn (and winning), my mother found beauty in what the world sees as an irritation.

Do you remember the time someone caused you to feel undesirable and you simply wanted to hide? Maybe you've been labeled as a problem or difficult to handle because of past failures or where you came from. How easily we invest in lies about our worth when we're not seeing ourselves through the eyes of our Creator. Solomon speaks to his beloved in Song of Solomon 4:7 that her beauty is complete. When we understand the Father's deep love for us, we can be assured that we are without blemish, flawless, and lacking nothing. Our security must be in He who sees our ugliest open wounds and insecurities and still calls us lovely. This is the audacious love of the Father, who sees in you what this world never will. Feel free to flourish, lion's tooth.

. . . .

BLOOM IS WHAT SHE WAS CREATED TO DO BLOOM IS WHAT SHE WILL

. . . .

LOVE

Chapter 2
Love

Do you want to be loved? Truly, before you read on, stop for a second and ask yourself, right now. You may have thought about it with the conclusive answer of "Yes!" Now to really stump your heart, sit back and think about *why* you want to be loved. To some, this can be a difficult question and to others, it may come quickly. (Feel free to close the book for pondering). Our craving for love is ignited by many things but truthfully, there isn't a single soul alive that doesn't want to be loved. It is one of the strongest, natural, emotional desires we have from infancy until death. If you came to a conclusion as to why you want to be loved, that's great! If you're not sure, that's great too. We were made from the love of God to love others.

The Origin of Love

Knowing that our lives are autographed by our Creator, we can identify our emotional roots in Him. Having flesh, the Son of God was in no way exempt from feeling every emotion you've ever felt. He cried at the death of His dear friend Lazarus (John 11:35). A whip-flailing Jesus felt anger at the moneychangers in the temple (John 2:15). Doubt whispered into his ears as He hung between heaven and earth on the cross (Mark 15:34). Fear left his lips as He prayed alone in the garden (Mark 14:36). Compassion filled his heart at the multitudes of the sick (Matthew 14:14). But the emotion I find most incredible is the love He felt for humanity while on earth. Jesus' radical sacrifice testifies of the Father's magnanimous mercy towards us. "For God so loved the world, that He gave his only begotten son, that whosoever believes in Him should not perish but have everlasting life." John 3:16 (KJV). These words tell the everyone that our Creator is so passionately in love with us, He abolished death *with* death through His Son, that He might have one chance to love us all a little closer one day. We're created in His love, now to extend it to others.

Love Gone Wrong?

"He loves me… He loves me not… He loves me… He loves me not… maybe it's for the better… I think I made a mistake…" We are the unrelenting hopeless romantics willing to do whatever it takes to love and be loved. With needle in hand, we sew our hearts to whatever conjures a smile. In the aspects of friendship, dating, and marriage, there has never been and never will be a "perfect relationship." If you're striving for one, save your heart the energy and rest. It's not going to happen for the simple fact that you and I are human and prone to really messing some things up. On the positive side, progressive and healthy relationships are devoid of constant criticism, jealousy, judgment, and mistrust. A healthy relationship will always bring out the best in a person, not conjure the worst.

Though you and I were created from love, there are times we find ourselves in these toxic relationships where wood floors are littered with eggshells and spilling ice cream on your shoes is more exciting than a walk in the park with your significant smother. This isn't love. We've all been there a time or two when the wrong thing is said to the wrong person and before long, we're scraping the remnants of "Word War III" off the walls. I believe our culture has assisted us with the confusion that began in the Garden, painting the image of dysfunctional relationships as common and even acceptable as long as we tolerate each other. We do ourselves a grand disservice by limiting relationships to a matter of toleration. I don't want to tolerate my wife, I want to love her. I do however tolerate things I have little power over such as influenza, bee stings, and other mishaps of life. Speak up! You deserve genuine, authentic love, not the lackluster, quasi-intimate, transactional love that we've (quite ironically) fallen in love with.

A Love Exhibition

To us, love is like an echo; we're far more inclined to give it when we're getting it. When John wrote this passage, he was using a Greek word for love, agape, which is a love not centered around what we get, but a love that gives. The record of Jesus' love is absolutely outlandish with its toes crossing boundaries many of us would be less inclined to breach today; a nondiscriminatory lavishing not merited by your color, economic status, health, or good deeds. It can't be won, and it can't be stolen. He loves you because you are simply you in all your glorious blemishes.

I can assure you that the most trying events in my life are those that have challenged me to demonstrate this agape love to others. It would be an absolute shame for me to tell you that such a demonstration comes naturally. That's called lying. Demonstrating love can be hard sometimes, especially when you've experienced deeply-rooted abuse, abandonment or heartache. What do you do when betrayal spray paints its name on the walls of your heart after daddy left? What remedy is there for the soul when a mere memory opens the bitter gates of hatred? Can forgiveness truly reign supreme in my heart? Between you and me, I believe it can, but I first must understand that Jesus is the conduit through which such love and forgiveness flow; it's not fully possible without Him. So, come! Grab your coat and a hot cup. Let's take a walk together and talk about the second facet of our journey: love, love, love.

> *"Dear friends, let us continue to love one another, for love comes from God. Anyone who loves is a child of God and knows God. But anyone who does not love does not know God, for God is love."*
>
> ***1 John 4:7-8 (NLT)***

Compass

Paths were perfect, planned, expected
'till her eyes caught Mr. Ected,
passing through the morning breeze,
beneath the copper maple trees.

Her fall for him, like autumn leaves
the homesick heart to grope.
Longing to be loved again
before a wending hope.

Linear and locked in place was life
before he saw the face of
sweet Ms. Guided wandering
the path he traveled, pondering.

He'd ache to miss love's catalyst
to life in fear alone,
so, unexpected Mr. Ected
walked Ms. Guided home.

> *"He who finds a wife, finds a treasure,*
> *and he receives favor from the LORD."*
>
> ***Proverbs 18:22 (NLT)***

Compass, a tale composed of compassion. It's the love story we all dream about, isn't it? Unexpectedly crossing paths with the love of our lives; the prelude to a perfect wedding in June where joy abounds, and the bride and groom leave immediately after the reception not to be heard from for weeks.

Now, this may not come to your surprise, but as long as you and I are human, we will love. No one has successfully made it out of life without experiencing some form of love. It's programmed into our human nature, and whether we like it or not (hopefully you do), we're going to fall for someone someday, but we must be aware that marriage is more than just another accomplishment, It's a covenant honored by God. Proverbs 18:22 states, "He who finds a wife, finds a treasure, and he receives favor from the LORD." The love a man feels for his wife is good! Such unity of a man with a woman is a reflection of Christ's love for the Church as stated in Ephesians 5:23: For the husband is the head of the wife, even as Christ is the head of the church: and He is the savior of the body. This union requires dedication and faithfulness, just as Christ is dedicated and faithful to us, the bride.

Let's segue for a moment. Remember the last time you came down with a case of influenza? The aches, belly-burbles, fever and chills? In order to remedy the ails, you probably ignored the symptoms and played a few rousing games of Parcheesi, right? No! You took care of your body with medicine, fluids, and lots of rest. Likewise, a man must care for his wife as he would his *own* body.

True love is shown through devotion, patience, and frequent checkups. Young men, when you find your wife, you truly have found a good thing. Just remember she was created to be part of you, so open the door of your heart and guide her home. Just be sure she's not Miss-Taken first.

- -

So. Unexpected Mr. ected walked Miss Guided home.

- -

Musings of the Master

Every note the Master writes
to simple hearts, like that of mine,
speaks promises of my Divine
for me to dine on finer wines and breads.

I take my Father's hand
and try to simplify His plans,
but nonetheless not understand
the worth He sees in me.

For this on faith, I choose to muse.
Be still my mind, do not peruse
and try with much futility
to peel apart the thoughts of Thee,
my Abba.

For my brain can't bend,
my mind too cramped to comprehend
Your cumbersome complexity and yet,
You're everything to me.

EDWARD HOLMES

You wove us ever careful
with the love You call Your hands.
Molding man from mirth and mud,
now this, I fail to understand.

We don't demand to be defined
but Lord you do it anyway.
Forever in your Kingdom, Lord
we lay, your sons to stay.

> *"When I look at the night sky and see the work of your fingers, the moon and the stars you set in place, what are mere mortals that you should think about them, human beings that you should care for them?"*
>
> ***Psalm 8:3-4 (NLT)***

The excitement we get from receiving a letter is somewhat of a forgotten joy for me. I remember writing letters to loved ones at a younger age, penning the "masterpiece" with the utmost care not to generate any mistakes. I am acquainted with many in my family who have been blessed with beautiful handwriting. Sadly, that isn't a gift I possess. My penmanship is something identical to a 5th grader's, yet nonetheless, a work in progress. When it was time to send a letter to someone special, careful consideration had to be taken for every word that graced the page: "Straight lines! Don't scribble! Be sure to utilize proper diction. After all, you don't want them to think you're a grammatic train wreck." Every careful stroke embodied the very emotions I struggled to convey in my young heart to its recipient.

In reflection, this is in many ways picturesque of the way our Heavenly Father desires to communicate with us: Carefully, intimately, laced with promise. The ultimate love-letter of our Creator, God-breathed, every jot and tittle, emphasis and extension fitly set for you and I today. His Word and promises endure forever (1 Peter 1:25).

His thoughts toward us are very good, and the richness of His wisdom is deeper than what we can fathom. It's today that we have access to the overwhelming reality of unmerited love that drives out fear. What are you waiting for? You've been invited to the table, so grab your letter-opener and rest in the eternal promises of a Kingdom that will never fade.

> Forever in your Kingdom, Lord,
> we lay, your sons to stay

Love On Display

I tried to buy love and it came in a box;
what a beautiful box with a bow!

I tore it apart, dug my fingers inside it
in search of a substance to show

my heart how to smile, it did for a *while*
but sooner or later I know

this feeling is fleeting, temporal and leaving
a hungrier void in my soul.

Oh, love's not a thing to be pulled from a box
or a shelf of material fixes.

Love is the answer, intangible and surely
what we've been hoping to witness

in a world full of hatred and falsified friendships.
It's everything we truly need.

So dig out your love from the heart, not a box
and lives will be changed
                             ...wait and see.

> *"Those who love money will never have enough. How meaningless to think that wealth brings true happiness!"*
>
> ***Ecclesiastes 5:10 (NLT)***

I like new things and so do you. There's something exciting about having a new experience! Not too long from now, your wireless carrier's going to release a fresh model of your current device and it'll have all the new bells and whistles you've been waiting for. Get ready to have a wider screen, more memory, a better camera, and even a few forgettable apps at your disposal! Since you're loyal and your screen is already cracked, you'll probably upgrade! After a few months, however, they're going to release the same phone, but this time you'll have new color varieties to choose from. You might not purchase it, but the temptation of novelty will present itself full force!

Research has shown that it's completely normal for us to have a problem with chasing that shiny new thing. When we have a new experience, the dopamine released actually motivates us to continue seeking rewards. This is what makes it hard to put down an immersive game after achieving a milestone. "Just one more round" could eventually turn into a sleepless night. I learned through experience that no matter how many things I purchase, they never truly made me happy. The hard drive with 200 questionably legal movies, albums or tickets to my favorite artist's shows were all surface-level fixes. I've spent a good portion of my past pursuing pathways to extrinsic happiness only to come up short time after time.

My friend, perhaps joy and happiness don't come from the things we fill our hands with, but perhaps the manner in which we extend them. We were commanded to love our brothers regardless of their intellect, appearance, or social class. We are to love others holistically and in doing so, we obtain much peace and satisfaction for living. So get up today! Turn off the negative newscast and kiss your anxieties goodbye! All you've ever been asked to do is love God and love people. Done.

LIVES WILL BE CHANGED
WAIT AND SEE

Harmony

Stepping from the curtain with
a palpitating heart,
his chest feels uncertain as
he stares into the dark.
He lifts his head with vacant eyes,
yet all that he can see
is where his partner used to stand
to sing his harmony.

Though shadows quite unsavory,
with bravery he clears
his throat to sing a duet, or
... a solo, it appears.
She wrote the song they sang together,
now he sings alone.
It wouldn't be the same but now
the show must still go on.

EDWARD HOLMES

It echoes through the rafters, touching
every vacant seat.
He struggles to sustain the notes,
the rhythm has him beat.
Yet, right before he walks off stage
a still small voice is heard,
it knows the verses, bridge and chorus,
every idle word.

Harmonious they sing the words
no man had ever known,
the lyrics of a friendship
deeply hidden, never shown.
With thunderous applause
and misty eyes, he takes a bow,
searching for the voice that knew
the lyrics then and now...

When loneliness like shadows seem
to capsulate your heart
Never walk by sight when you
emerge to sing your part.
Lift your head and know that you
are one and He is Three
The Living God is always there
to sing your harmony.

> "For the LORD your God is living among you. He is a mighty savior. He will take delight in you with gladness. With His love, He will calm all your fears. He will rejoice over you with joyful songs."
>
> ***Zephaniah 3:17 (NLT)***

Have you ever cried out for help only to hear the echoes of your distress? Not a friend or loved one near to lift your heart when you've needed it most? Isolation is something that we've all experienced at one point or another. Fueled by fear, isolation tells us that we've no one to advocate for us; that we are completely and utterly alone in our situation.

There's an account in Genesis 16 about a woman named Hagar, Sarai's Egyptian servant. Sarai, being barren, suggested to her husband Abram that she might bear a child through her maidservant, Hagar. After conceiving a child, Hagar no longer gave respect to Sarai, which resulted in removal from their estate. Hagar began to run hard from Sarai's face! Rejected and broken without anyone to lean on, she took rest by a fountain in the wilderness. Just when she thought no one else could see her pain and plight, God stepped in to reassure her of His plan for her life.

(Genesis 16:10). With a heart swelled with gladness, she praised Him as El Roi, "The God who sees me."

The next moment your broken heart aches for someone to simply see into your situation, remember that He does! He sees the amazing version of you that you wish your family could understand. He sees you when shame has overtaken and the first thing you want to do is hide. He sees your joys, successes, and promotions. He is El Roi! Just as with Hagar, God's eyes are always upon you and there is nothing that could ever separate you from His Love (Romans 8:39). So when you feel like you've been singing the same solo for years, put your trust in God. He's still there.

The Living God is always there to sing your harmony

Through the Loop

When you can't
but you've tried
very hard
day and night
so you say
"Maybe so"
things untie
but you sew
so you pray
"Father God, is it right, or is it not?"
—No reply
so you wait
then you try to separate
but you can't
and you've tried
very hard
day and night
so you say
"Maybe so"
things untie
but you sew.

> *"As a dog returns to his vomit, so a fool repeats his foolishness."*
>
> ***Proverbs 26:11 (NLT)***

How easy is it to find ourselves in circumstances that we don't need to be in? It's usually within the quiet moments of the evening, wide-eyed in the darkness, that your choices start to sink in. "Oh... did I *really* agree to that?" If you find yourself wearing a t-shirt from the "Bad Decision Makers Club," fear not, my friend, you're not alone.

The biblical figure Samson delivers great intrigue (Judges 16:4-22). After losing his wife to a tragic attack led by the Philistines facilitated by vengeance, his eyes were captivated by a woman named Delilah. Together, they created a dissonant mixture of dogged lust and an eleven-hundred silver piece Philistine paycheck. What love! Three times this mighty man of God deceived her, well-knowing her scheme of finding the roots of his power, but his ego led to his downfall. Samson adamantly clutched onto his bad company in Delilah until one night she gained the upper-hand and got "a head" in the game of love.

When tied up from toxic choices, keep calm and cut the cord. The more we continuously flirt with dangerous choices, the less we should marvel when they bind our hands to hold us captive again and again. We will fail and fall short standing toe to toe with temptations, fully reliant on our own strength. Leave the seams of your heart to the Omnipotent Outfitter (Psalm 147:3). Before you sew, let it go, lest you lose sight of your identity.

Don't do it, Fido! It'll only taste worse the third time.

THINGS UNTIE BUT YOU SEW

Senseless

Scarlet hands that gripped the fence
were mine, but now I couldn't sense
the piercing winds that chapped my soul.
That night I fled the gates of home.

I heard your love would e'er be kind,
yet sin's deceptions kissed the mind.
In haste, I cup my ears from Thee.
The night I fled, You beckoned me.

Waters fog the scenery
of snows and streak the weary cheek
with salted stains of solemn grief.
The night I fled, You sought for me.

Odiferous, the burden held
upon my back began to smell
of pungent pride and self-pity.
The night I fled, I couldn't breathe.

I fall and taste my ill repute,
expelling pride to live for you.
Slowly sickened, sore from sin.
The night I fled, You took me in.

FINGERPRINTS OF LOVE & WAR

> *"His son said to him, 'Father, I have sinned against both heaven and you, and I am no longer worthy of being called your son.'"*
>
> ***Luke 15:21 (NLT)***

"EVERYBODY, CALM DOWN! I got this!" If you're anything like me, you've probably expressed your incredible ability to dive into action and take the helm! Of course, you are! We're capable, strong, and desire independence because you and I know best, right? We know what to do in a pinch, swimming upstream against the chilly flow like a mighty, self-sufficient salmon. Okay, let's be honest with ourselves for a moment if that's alright. There are times when you and I are the farthest from being strong and maybe we're not as independent as we claim to be. Come to think of it, we're really not that good at going against the current all the time, and stepping out on our own has led to trouble a time or two. I think I would make a pretty poor salmon—a quivering, co-dependent salmon.

Sometimes we choose our own path and stray far from the hands that provide for us. The poem Senseless is built from those seasons in life when we crown ourselves captains of our souls. Jesus tells a parable about two sons. One squandered all his bountiful inheritance on women, parties, and wasteful living. Eventually, he returned home empty, afraid, and guilt-ridden. No doubt, the father knew his son had strayed away from all moral stabilities instilled throughout his life; yet instead of chastising his son for straying, the father sees to it that the son is robed, embraced, and welcomed through the door as if he had never left. Here's my take-away: The Father in Jesus' parable had only one concern that day - his son's homecoming. The women? Overlooked. The money? Never mentioned. Weeks without a shower? Not part of the conversation! Drop the duffel bag, beloved, the Father is running your way…

SLOWLY SICKENED, SORE FROM SIN.
THE NIGHT I FLED, YOU TOOK ME IN.

Why the Kettle Sings

I'm convinced...
        that God loves tea.
                Please hear me.

You took me as I am:
a mess of a man, gathered by the hands
of Jesus,
son-dried and oxidized now
baptized & optimized for sapid savor.

Flavor was
forced from my frail fibers
while my heart was slowly
steeped in heat deep down like
bold black teas. I call it poetry. These

p r i v a t e

soliloquies once secretly steaming,
now publicly poured-out praise,
aromatic to the nasals of the Ancient of Days.

I'll gladly raise my cup.

And if it's the fire that draws out the best of me,
I now know why the kettle sings.

> *"So be truly glad. There is wonderful joy ahead, even though you must endure many trials for a little while. O that the tested genuineness of your faith—more precious than gold that perishes though it is tested by fire—may be found to result in praise and glory and honor at the revelation of Jesus Christ."*
>
> ***1 Peter 1:6-7 (NLT)***

I waited to watch the wood begin to glow from within the fireplace before me, knowing soon the kindling would be the stage for flames to dance! Oxygen coaxed their madness while embers yawned deep from the belly of the brick-base. Within moments... heat transformed what lay within to ash. It was then that I questioned God if He could do the same for me.

We see a recurring theme of fire represented as an agent of purification in biblical texts. The written and spoken words of God are referenced as fire in John 15:3 and Jeremiah 23:29. The Spirit of God is referenced as fire in Acts 2:3 and the Father is described as an all-consuming fire in Hebrews 12:29. I believe this is worth noting because of the literal properties of physical fire in tandem with spiritual and metaphoric fire. If kindled, flames can sustain life, illuminate, consume, and purify. This is also true for our Creator.

It's my hope in this journey with you, that the flames of your situation draw out the very best. It may be uncomfortable and even unbearable at times, but we can find personal growth and hope even when the furnace of our life is turned up ten times hotter than it's ever been. Every ounce of rejection, sickness, shame and torment you've been facing is going to produce your finest flavor in due time, so let your life be a sweet savor in the face of the Father.

I'LL GLADLY RAISE MY CUP

WAR

Chapter 3
War

On The Outside

Conflict can be externally generated. Our individual lives are like strokes of paint on a canvas; radiant hues of reds and blues blended together to create a portrait of His glory. It's a masterpiece of individually unique bodies with unique thoughts. Though diverse, our eccentricities can either generate complement or contrast. Often we experience the latter more prevalently because of our differences. Unfortunately, gender, social status, and culture tend to divide us and breed opposition towards one another. This is the face of oppression, bullying, and divorce, where external conflict yells while compassion crumbles.

The Inner Me

How do we classify internal conflicts? Well, that's simple. These are the wars that we fight within ourselves when our train of thought is chugging 60 miles a second, and the brakes stopped working half a mile before Decision Street. You and I will find ourselves toe-to-toe with life-altering decisions that require us to carefully calculate the best roads to travel in life. The good news is that internal conflicts are absolutely normal and as we live, we'll experience such a disconnect from time to time.

We all war within ourselves about much, but it's important to remember that each day is founded upon *choice*. The mature believer must make up his/her mind to walk towards the things that add value to their life. Seeking the wisdom of Christ is a *choice*. Holiness as a lifestyle is a *choice*. Seeking help to break generational bonds of addiction, alcoholism, and fear, are all choices we make for a better inner me.

Active Duty

Sometimes that conflict is with the spiritual aspect of our lives: facing the fight in the furnace of our faith –a place where the legitimacy of our walk with God is tried and our preparation to apply the Word of God becomes evident. We discover through His Word that the battles we fight are not always of a tangible nature but are of a spiritual one. This would mean that there are adversities we face which are triggered more by who we are spiritually than who we are physically. To paraphrase Jesus, we are as citizens of heaven, to never get caught up by worldly snares (John 17:16). Even further, the Word commands us that getting caught up in the lifestyle of a civilian prohibits the believer from truly pleasing the Master (2 Timothy 2:4). Fighting against sinful snares every day is evidence that a man desires the riches of heaven.

Winning Team

So here we are, in the middle of the war zone, face to face with opposition and your peace of mind is at stake. We can't live sober-minded when we're lambasted on every side by opposition, so what do we do? We fight! We fight in the physical for freedom. We speak up and speak out for those who cannot speak for themselves. We pursue the undeserved grace and reconciliation given to us through Christ and rise up on weak knees even in the midst of moral shortcomings. We remind ourselves that we are the head and not the tail and

should never settle for less than who we're created to be. And most importantly of all, my friend, we pray. We pray knowing that now is not forever and every pain hurt has an expiration date. We pray because deliverance dwells in true travail. We pray because the battle is not ours, and never was… It is the LORD'S! Come! Let's make war,
it's in our blood!

Focus

I've seen broken people in
a million different places,
broken hearts behind the smiles
on a multitude of faces.

Men are masking mangled memories
in all the broken spaces of the places
fear erased the hope
disparity replaces.

How I pray these broken brothers
with their burdens and their woes
could find the missing peace they've lost
within their troubled souls.

By now you might be wondering
how one can see the truth.
Darling, you can spot the broken folk if
you've been broken too.

> *"If we claim we have no sin, we are only fooling ourselves and not living in the truth."*
>
> ***I John 1:8***

Fell down ~~one flight~~ two flights of stairs? Done. Hand slammed in the car door? Check. What about the time you rocked moist socks to work because they weren't dry by the time you had to leave… no? Just me? OK., great! Hello imperfect reader, I believe we're in good company… There's some tea in the kitchen, I believe we've quite a bit to discuss.

Have you ever tried to practice perfection? It's an exciting concept based on that lie that what you do, is and will never be good enough. In a nutshell, it's self-rejection in exchange to perpetuate the worship of man's opinion. It's almost to say "Others notice what I do, therefore my existence is validated."

At one point in my life, I truly believed that our Father could love me more if I *did* more. As if the words "It is finished" were the prologue to the Book of Works forwarded by M. Y. Pride. It was a mindset that acknowledged the presence of God's love but believed that it could somehow be modified. It didn't take long to realize that I was wrong. The glaring problem lies in the fact that we're human and ever prone to folly, therefore we can put no full trust in ourselves. It's foolish to believe that we're perfect people who always hit the mark and never trip in our walk.

Therefore, we can only trust in the security of God's faithfulness and the completed work of Christ in crucifixion. You're going to receive some scars in life before your story wraps up, and the most oddly comforting fact is knowing that I will too. I've got extra bandages if you need them.

DARLING, YOU CAN SPOT THE BROKEN FOLK IF YOU'VE BEEN BROKEN, TOO.

Edge

He stands in the valley, domain of the dead,
the cries of the fallen draw near.
Each grave is a tally of all the blood shed.
His hand slowly trembles with fear.

The air teems with tension, the demons they dance
thrashing wild with unbridled elation.
In this dissension he readies his stance
pressing forward without hesitation.

The bodies, a multitude file behind him.
A legion afflicted with sin.
The clang of their shackles are heard from afar.
The pound of his heart beats within.

Then darkness descends, so thick you can feel it
as chills rip the air like a knife.
A dark figure bends from the depths of the valley
as the demons bow down in the night.

Slender and serpentine up from the shadows
the enemy stares with dismay
at the helpless in bondage, he looms high above them
unhinging his jawbone to say:

EDWARD HOLMES

"Disgusting, unworthy, unlovable lot.
You've all fallen short of the glory of God.
You're putrid, unfaithful, your life is for naught.
Your bodies would find better purpose to rot.

Tongues praise your 'king,' then curse with the same?
You hypocrite, foolhardy, children of shame!
Bitterness holds you, you can't walk away.
Your past is your bondage, you might as well stay.

Your mouths made for scorning and eyes made for lust.
The King that you serve is a God you can't trust.
Your hands trained for murder drip red with your guilt.
You can't run away from the blood that you've spilt.

Your flesh is your chamber, carnality craves.
Your pine for fulfillment makes way to your grave.
God cannot forgive you, so why do you try?
Draw closer to me, ye shall not surely die."

Sober and vigilant ready to strike,
the crowd to his back cry in pain.
His mind on a mission, he raises his head
hand gripping the blade unashamed.

FINGERPRINTS OF LOVE & WAR

His eyes lock the enemy, bitter and callous,
the sword in the midst of the fray.
Directing the steel to the enemy's brow,
he steps toward the devil to say:

"My God is a God of omnipotent power,
His grace like a hurricane force.
His voice like the ocean, His eyes glow with fire,
His love: an unstoppable source.

The Word of my Father is living and quick,
pure and convicting and whole.
A light to my path and a lamp to my feet
and it severs the marrow and soul.

Touch NOT the anointed for righteous are they,
it is written that blessed are the meek.
It is written that blessed are the thirsty and pure,
for blessed are my brothers you seek.

Worthless and sinful are things you accuse them,
we've all fallen short, this YOU know.
But you're quick to reform, twist, contort and confuse
them and strike when my brethren are low.

EDWARD HOLMES

The poison you whisper convince the afflicted.
You pick at their wounds like a crow.
Dead are the tares of confusion you spread
and you've nothing but falsehood to show.

Though captive were they, their bondage is broken,
we're free by the blood of the Lamb.
No rulers of darkness can touch His anointed,
so Satan, I'm taking my stand!

It is written His coming is soon to behold,
minute hands prophesy your demise.
I will reign, in the name of the almighty King
and I'll fight till His glory arrives!"

The demons, they shriek with unparalleled terror
as shadows were caked with their masses.
The blade pointed high toward the father of lies
with the power no shadow surpasses.

Left through the air, silver gleam to the right
with the sword, every corner exposed.
Not a bond nor a chain could be found in the light,
not even that serpent of old.

FINGERPRINTS OF LOVE & WAR

So He walked through the valley,
the land of the living
with shouts of the captive made free

by the quickening pages;
the Edges of Ages
which liberate you

…even me.

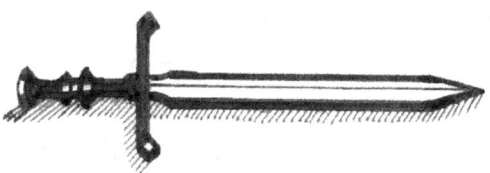

> *"I will give him the honors of a victorious soldier, because he exposed himself to death. He was counted among the rebels. He bore the sins of many and interceded for rebels."*
>
> ***Isaiah 53:12 (NLT)***

Everyone needs a hero. Isn't it hard to experience life when you feel like no one will stand up for you? How about intercede for you in the midst of trouble? Intercede? Intercede comes from the Latin word intercedere; "inter" meaning to "be between," while "cedere" means to "go." Intercession simply means to "go in-between two opposing things." It has to do with your position. I like to think of it as a hero swooping in to defend the weak in the midst of a heated battle, taking the brunt of every attack to save a life. That's a true hero!

> *This High Priest of ours understands our weaknesses, for He faced all of the same testings we do, yet He did not sin.*
> *Hebrews 4:15 (NLT)*

For us to receive salvation, we needed someone who could identify with our iniquities and plead for our righteousness. Christ embodied sin, conquered it and now stands in the gap for us daily as our great intercessor. Because of Jesus, we have a mighty defender who can empathize with our anxieties, temptations, depression, and doubt. We have an advocate who understands us when our own families forsake us and our friends abandon us. We have a Hero. A Hero who already defeated our enemies.

> NOT A BOND NOR A CHAIN
> COULD BE FOUND IN THE LIGHT
> NOT EVEN THAT SERPENT OF OLD

Last Word

His books were all gathered,
the classroom dispersed,
the bell rang, commencing round four.
Who would have thought he would give up tonight
since nobody witnessed the war?

Fear gripped his chest as he stepped through the hall.
Phrases of scorn echoed off every wall,
into his ears flooding down to his core,
yet nobody witnessed the war.

Wounded yet smiling, playing the part,
taking each blow with a warrior's heart.
Their heavy words were like fiery darts,
yet nobody witnessed the war.

They never saw past the jokes with their friends.
Their vocal sepulchers were burying him.
Inside he's wounded but forced to pretend,
yet nobody witnessed the war.

EDWARD HOLMES

To the school he's a geek and a freak, a degenerate,
ugly and queer, overweight but he's innocent!
They called him filthy, but God made him clean,
yet nobody witnessed the war.

So they pierced him with prejudice,
lashed him with labels.
Picked up and moved when he sat at their tables.
Lied and denied any affiliation.
Bullying back was a constant temptation,

but he never did so instead he grew sore.
He needed a hero, but no one came forth.
Who would have thought he would give up tonight,
since nobody witnessed the war...

> *"The tongue can bring death or life; those who love to talk will reap the consequences."*
>
> ***Proverbs 18:21 (NLT)***

Many men have mouths made like mausoleums; devoid of life. They abound in death, delivering destruction through degenerate diction. In my life, I have been both the bully and the bullied. As a child, I was temperamental and very self-conscious. Naturally, the best way to relieve my insecurities was to point out the flaws in someone else. I launched insults, rapid fire like they were going out of style, ignoring the brokenness within the offended. Fortunately, God has a wonderful way of working, and I found myself on the tail end of the spectrum in high school. The medicine was bitter, but it opened up my eyes to the power of positive words.

This is the amazing part where you and I come in! Scripture tells us that "The tongue can bring death or life; those who love to talk will reap the consequences." (Proverbs 18:21 NLT). Thousands of our country's youth take their lives every year as a result of verbal abuse. They're looking for someone to give them a reason. We have the seeds of life and death…of which do we plant? Someone somewhere is waiting for you to remind them that they still matter. All it takes is one person; all it takes is you. What are you waiting for? Speak up for those who cannot speak for themselves; ensure justice for those being crushed. Proverbs 31:8 (NLT)

What are your words doing in their minds right now?

> Their heavy words were like fiery darts.

Still Water

How long have you been fighting, child
do they know you're winded?
How long has God been silent, son
and sympathy suspended?
How many years, the battering
has left you undefended?
Has it ended?
Just pretend it
didn't happen,
all is well.

How much foundation does it take
to cover up the blue?
How long will it be safer just
to stay in solitude?
How many times accused of crimes,
abused behind the doors?
Will the victim
then convict him
or convince them…
all is well?

EDWARD HOLMES

I have to keep it secret here
they told me not to utter.
And if a soul discovers
first we'll lie, then tell another.
"I'm fine, is what I'll whisper,
"Set me free!" the inner yell.
You knew but never drew
from deeper water in the well.

> *"Fearing people is a dangerous trap, but trusting the LORD means safety."*
>
> ***Proverbs 29:25 (NLT)***

Our childhood home holds memories from wall to wall, ceiling to floor. Growing up was a universe of discovery for a young mind. With an overactive imagination, my bedroom, at any given moment, would transform from a playroom to a bounce house (until something broke, of course).

Children have an incredible way of misusing valuable things. As peculiar as it sounds, one of the best ways to pass time—usually during timeout—was playing with the secret golden spring on the wall. "Boing!... thud-d-d-d" What humor! "Boing!...thud-d-d-d." It never got old. I remember its final huzzah when it broke without hope of repair. No, I didn't tell my parents, I couldn't even spell "obituary." So, I left it alone, never realizing it was meant to stop the door until the handle busted a hole in the wall. *They found out.* In the same way, we interact and even use others around us in ways that they weren't created to be used. Abuse is a very real, very pervasive part of humanity and has taken form emotionally, financially, physically and even digitally. We tear each other down with our words, bruise innocent trust with our hands and manipulate the ignorant with lies. Many live on the receiving end of abuse from peers, family, or strangers without uttering a sound. Many will live with secrets their whole lives out of fear of what would happen if they're ever bold enough to utter a sound. If you have never worked as a gemologist or gem appraiser, you cannot determine the legitimate value of a gemstone. It takes a master to determine true color, cut, carat, and clarity for proper appraisal.

God's Word tells us that his people will be as precious stones of a crown (Zechariah 9:16). We wouldn't be in error to believe that's you and me, not priced less but priceless. Regardless of the situation, you must remember that what happened to you in that season is not your fault, for children... have an incredible way of misusing *valuable things*.

"I'M FINE" IS WHAT I WHISPER
"SET ME FREE" THE INNER YELL

Wrinkles

I'm thinking that I'm capable,
significant and free.
I'm thinking I'll accomplish
what is set in front of me.
I'm thinking I'm professional,
astute and full of charm,
so what's the matter thinking, friend?
Oh, what could be the harm?

I'm thinking I'm a failure,
my job's an awful shame.
I'm thinking I'll fall short of
everything I plan to gain.
I'm thinking I'm a vagabond,
that's all I'll ever be.
So what's the matter thinking friend?
What harm is it to me?

Well…

EDWARD HOLMES

The mind's a tricky fellow
with a knack for sleight-of-hand;
A prestidigitator
that can change the views of man.
Your life can be a great success
or wracked by daily grief.
You are the thoughts of yesterday.
What harm could thinking be?

To think a thought is trifle
is a trifle thought to think;
a trivial assumption for
the life you plan to lead.
So as we purpose in our heart,
we think and so are we.
You are the thoughts of yesterday.
What harm could thinking be?

> *"And now, dear brothers and sisters, one final thing. Fix your thoughts on what is true, and honorable, and right, and pure, and lovely, and admirable. Think about things that are excellent and worthy of praise."*
>
> **Philippians 4:8 (NLT)**

One of the greatest wars that could ever be fought is taking place right now between the "temple walls" of your head. I can hear the clash of steel echo through the hallways of my thoughts around the corridors and doors that ask for more of my innocent intrigue. It is a mental mutiny conspired by fears once subordinated, now on the forefront of my life fighting for attention. Truth versus lies, amorality against morality, and here we stand in the midst of it all. It's ultimately up to you and I to decide who wins. Each day we oscillate back and forth between what we know is pure and what isn't. Personally, I fight a losing battle with the healthy food group of donuts and coffee daily, there's no question about it. Some thoughts are weighty and some are not. The way we think about ourselves and the culture around us can affect how we live our lives.

This is where the Word comes into view. We're told that, "as a man thinks in his heart so is he…" (Proverbs 23:7). This is to say that our actions and demeanor are usually a reflection of whatever we've been thinking about. I act on what I believe about myself. You and I are more inclined to vocalize what we've diligently rehearsed in our minds. There will be days when destructive memories slip into your mind to drag you back to where you've planted a flag of freedom. These days will come, but know this: bitterness, and flashbacks of abuse *can* be rendered powerless. You are not a bystander! The authority to topple every lie that dares to cross the line is yours. Can you hear it? Steel to steel. Thought to thought. Your victories may just be one mindset away.

WHAT HARM COULD THINKING BE?

Temperance

Miriam! Miriam! Manage your monster,
that terrible beast from the chambers you keep.
The key was found broken. The bars were all bent
and the curtains we hung last December were rent.

I followed it down into town as it terrified
bankers, the bakers and barbers and then it tried
burning the bridges so no one could come inside,
few could escape it, survive it or hide.

I watched as it severed the closest of friends
with its razor-like tongue as it buckled and bent
through the streets over buses, pedestrians, carriages,
leveling churches and severing marriages.

Barreling! Barreling! Belching up bitterness
into the atmosphere, darker than licorice.
Blinding the eyes of compassion and vigilance,
hindering hearts as a master of dissonance.

Miriam! Miriam! Manage your anger,
that terrible beast from the chambers you keep.
It's back in captivity, far from humanity,
promise me darling, you'll tame it this week?

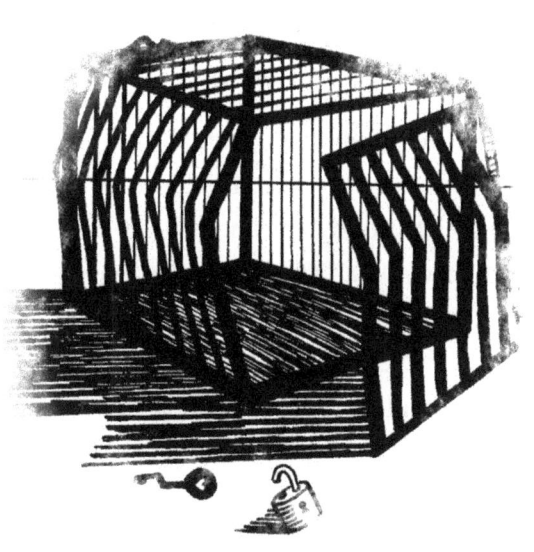

> *"My dear brothers and sister, take note of this: Everyone should be quick to listen, slow to speak and slow to become angry, because human anger does not produce the righteousness that God desires."*
>
> ***James 1:19-20 (NLT)***

Every vein in his temple pounds past his furrowed brow. Tread lightly if you can! Whatever you say next is bound to be grossly misunderstood. After all, he's right, you know. In fact, he's never wrong and he's made that clear a few times in the past. As long as your exit over the eggshell-laden floor is flawless this month, you should avoid yet another domestic war.

We all know someone with a short fuse and an alibi. It almost seems as though they've got a better relationship with anger than with you, and God forbid you come between them. Sadly, anger can come from different places such as feelings of injustice, vulnerability and hurt to name a few. As unfortunate as these may be, uncontrollable anger can have damaging effects on relationships of every kind. The biblical patriarch Moses had several instances where anger rose to the occasion: He was angry at Israel for the worship of idols, committed murder and even broke two of the tablets given to him by God. Eventually we see these fits of rage climax when Moses disobeys specific direction from God to speak to a rock that would provide water for the people of Israel (Numbers 20:8). He did not obey, but in his frustration, calls the people rebels, sarcastically asks if it is he who must bring the water, then strikes the rock twice before the congregation. Moses died without having a chance to step foot into the Promised Land for which his very life was based upon obtaining, a land overflowing with prosperity and provision. We should always be careful not to allow a spirit of anger to arise in the chambers of our hearts. After all, you and I may have a few cities to rebuild if we're not careful.

PROMISE ME DARLING,
YOU'LL TAME IT THIS WEEK?

Fetter Pillows

In the chamber, myrrh and aloe
rest beneath Deception's face.
Grins impress her pillows right
from where she lies
today

between the fabric-
ated stories, writhing 'tween
the comfort spread.
Darling, must we skirt the issue
seeing how you've made your bed?

Her golden lockes are bronze, my son,
so carry not the key,
as such will lead a man to death
and rend thy soul from thee.

But hearken unto wisdom,
as she calls aloud, you'll see.
Her love is life.
Her love is light.
Her love is liberty.

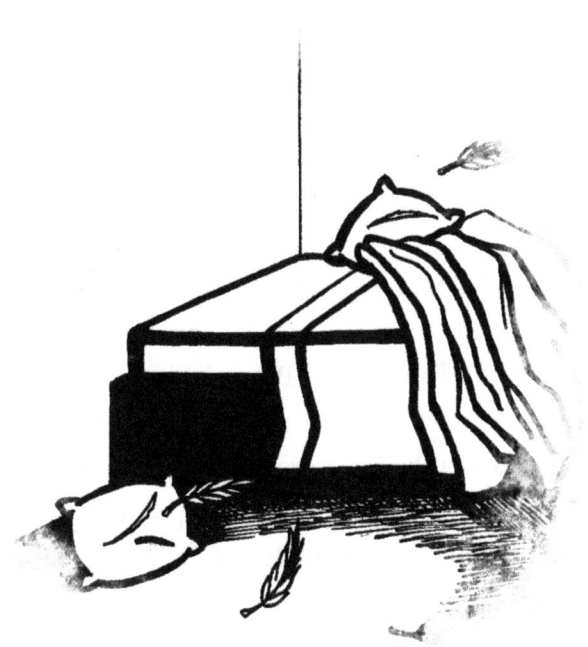

> *"My bed is spread with beautiful blankets, with colored sheets of Egyptian linen. I've perfumed my bed with myrrh, aloes, and cinnamon. Come, let's drink our fill of love until morning. Let's enjoy each other's caresses, for my husband is not home. He's away on a long trip."*
>
> ***Proverbs 7:16-19 (NLT)***

"What have I done? Everybody probably knows by now. But what if they don't? Am I ... am I able to cover the evidence!?" The book of Proverbs is comprised of wisdom and instruction. Chapter seven tells a story of a young man who had been roaming the night streets. He got wrapped up in the embrace of promiscuity and a woman not only invites him home, but into the finest bedroom of the hour. The snare was set, and although previous warning had been given (Proverbs 5:20), conviction was captured by the craves of concupiscence.

Many have been captured by the allures of sexual enticements tethered on threads of taciturn temptations. Just as stealthily do these enticements catch us off guard and as soon as a second glance is allowed to take root, it can pierce a heart through with arrows of crippling shame. Sexually related struggles have a **powerful** grip on the mind if never confronted. This is how what King David handled it:

"When I refused to confess my sin, my body wasted away, and I groaned all day long. Day and night your hand of discipline was heavy on me. My strength evaporated like water in the summer heat. Finally, I confessed all my sins to you and stopped trying to hide my guilt. I said to myself 'I will confess my rebellion to the Lord.' And you forgave me! All my guilt is gone." (Psalm 32:3-5 NLT)

Winning the war against the shame that follows sexual struggles starts with humility and confession: confession that we are far too frail to fight the foe before us. We are not created to carry the weight of shame so if you're able, beloved, take the other street.

- - -

DARLING, MUST WE SKIRT THE ISSUE SEEING HOW YOU'VE MADE YOUR BED?

- - -

Final Word

Until this point, we've been on sort of a journey, haven't we? A journey of *purpose*, knowing that we are His workmanship, created in Jesus Christ for good works that God has already ordained. We find that our identity as vessels for His Glory are found hidden in Christ and not the temporary pleasures of this world.

A journey of Love where we can bask in the reality that we are products of His Love – a love that covers every stain of transgression and sees beauty in the desolate, defiled parts of our lives and pursues us still. We can walk confidently knowing that our adoration comes not from what we DO, but simply for who we are.

A Journey of warfare that reminds us of the power to defend what we know is good, right and true - to stand up for those who cannot speak for themselves and rise above substandard ways of living. Raise your banner high, the war is already won and you are free to walk in victory.

My Friend,

I pray that you have the strength to walk in newness and revelation of who you were created to be each day. Let 2 Corinthians 5:17 be evident as you bear a new name in Jesus, no longer identified by the past but alive in Christ. May your reputation in the Kingdom of Heaven be known by your adoption (Galatians 4:6). I pray that the Love of God be shed abroad in your heart, rekindling hope and covering shame that so easily lingers in our lives. Let the unmerited, unrelenting love of the Father overtake and overflow into every area of your life. Lord, as we allow You to love us, help us to demonstrate this love to one another. Only then will we see your Kingdom manifested on earth as it is in Heaven. I pray that you have the vitality to fight just one more day. Let your strength be found in Him as you walk through life this side of Heaven. Lord, grant us a boldness to say what You've called us to say and do only what You've called us to do in whatever capacity You desire. Finally, as we come to a close…

"You are His handiwork and He is your lifeline. You are the dust behind each nail a testimony of His careful craftsmanship. He's ready for your next move, are you?"

Edward Holmes is an American author and speaker with an evangelist's heart and a poetic pen.
It's his life mission to encourage others that the darkest corners are life are *still* worth living through his writing, ministry and speaking engagements.

You can connect with him and his work on:

Instagram: @Edwardlee_on_ig
Facebook:@Edwardlee423
Twitter: @EdwardHolmes11

EDWARD HOLMES

YOU MAY ALSO ENJOY

My first full-length poetry book.
It's heart fuel from me to you.

NOW AVAILABLE THROUGH
ONLINE BOOKSELLERS

www.ingramcontent.com/pod-product-compliance
Lightning Source LLC
Chambersburg PA
CBHW071848090426
42811CB00004B/530